My First Animal Library

Hyenas

by Penelope S. Nelson

Bullfrog Books

Ideas for Parents and Teachers

Bullfrog Books let children practice reading informational text at the earliest reading levels. Repetition, familiar words, and photo labels support early readers.

Before Reading

- Discuss the cover photo. What does it tell them?
- Look at the picture glossary together. Read and discuss the words.

Read the Book

- "Walk" through the book and look at the photos. Let the child ask questions. Point out the photo labels.
- Read the book to the child, or have him or her read independently.

After Reading

- Prompt the child to think more. Ask: Have you heard about hyenas before reading this book? What more would you like to learn about them after reading it?

Bullfrog Books are published by Jump!
5357 Penn Avenue South
Minneapolis, MN 55419
www.jumplibrary.com

Library of Congress Cataloging-in-Publication Data

Names: Nelson, Penelope, 1994– author.
Title: Hyenas / by Penelope S. Nelson.
Description: Bullfrog books edition.
Minneapolis, MN : Jump!, Inc., [2020]
Series: My first animal library
Audience: Age 5–8. | Audience: K to Grade 3.
Includes index.
Identifiers: LCCN 2018038343 (print)
LCCN 2018039069 (ebook)
ISBN 9781641285575 (ebook)
ISBN 9781641285568 (hardcover : alk. paper)
Subjects: LCSH: Hyenas—Juvenile literature.
Classification: LCC QL737.C24 (ebook)
LCC QL737.C24 N45 2020 (print)
DDC 599.74/3—dc23
LC record available at https://lccn.loc.gov/2018038343

Editor: Jenna Trnka
Designer: Jenna Casura

Photo Credits: rujitop/Can Stock Photo, cover; Enrique Ramos/Shutterstock, 1; francesco de marco/Shutterstock, 3; Daniel-Alvarez/Shutterstock, 4; Biosphoto/SuperStock, 5; Joe McDonald/Getty, 6–7, 23tm; Anup Shah/Age Fotostock, 8–9, 23bm; Ariadne Van Zandbergen/Alamy, 10–11; Vladimir Wrangel/Shutterstock, 12; Eric Isselee/Shutterstock, 13; Bridgena BArnard /Shutterstock, 14–15, 23br; robertharding/Alamy, 16–17, 23tl; belizar/Shutterstock, 18, 23tr; Suzi Eszterhas/Minden Pictures/SuperStock, 19, 23bl; MicheleB/Shutterstock, 20–21; Aaron Amat/Shutterstock, 22; Simoneemanphotography/iStock, 24.

Printed in the United States of America at Corporate Graphics in North Mankato, Minnesota.

Table of Contents

Hyenas Hunt

What is
that sound?

It sounds
like a laugh.

It is a hyena!

It found prey.

It lets the clan know.

Clans are big.

How many are in one?

As many as 80!

Wow!

clan

The clan hunts together.

Why?

To get big prey.

Like zebras. Or antelope.

One can hunt alone, too.

It hunts fish.

What else?

Other small animals.

Food left by others.

Many have spots on their fur.

Some have stripes.

They fight.

Why?

To move up in rank.

alpha

The alpha is female.

She eats first.

Nice!

Moms have cubs.
How many?
Up to four.

They live in a den.

Cool!

They grow up.
Some stay with mom.
Some leave.

Parts of a Hyena

ears
Hyenas have great hearing to help them hunt.

nose
Hyenas have an excellent sense of smell, which helps them find food.

neck
Hyenas have strong necks for carrying prey.

teeth and jaw
Hyenas have very strong teeth and jaws. They eat all parts of their prey, except the horns! They have the strongest bite of any mammal.

legs
A hyena's front legs are longer than its back legs.

paw
Each paw has four toes with claws that help catch prey.

Picture Glossary

alpha
The top hyena in a clan.

clan
A group of hyenas.

cubs
Young hyenas.

den
The home of a wild animal.

prey
An animal that is eaten by other animals for food.

rank
A level or position in a group.

Index

To Learn More

Finding more information is as easy as 1, 2, 3.

1. Go to www.factsurfer.com
2. Enter "hyenas" into the search box.
3. Click the "Surf" button to see a list of websites.